THE PROPHET OF
BERKELEY SQUARE

Borgo Press Books by FRANK J. MORLOCK

The Chevalier d'Éon and Other Short Farces from the Eighteenth- and Nineteenth-Century French Theatre (Editor)
Chuzzlewit
Congreve's Comedy of Manners
Crime and Punishment
Falstaff (with William Shakespeare, John Dennis, and William Kendrick)
Fathers and Sons
The Idiot
Jurgen
Justine
Lord Jim
The Molière Plays (Editor)
Notes from the Underground
Oblomov
Old Creole Days
Outrageous Women: Lady Macbeth and Other French Plays (editor and translator)
Peter and Alexis
The Princess Casamassima
The Prophet of Berkeley Square
A Raw Youth
The Stendhal Hamlet Scenarios and Other Shakespearean Shorts from the French (editor and translator)
Two Voltairean Plays: The Triumvirate and Comedy at Ferney (editor)
The Widow's Husband; and, Porthos in Search of an Outfit: Two Dumasian Comedies (editor and translator)

THE PROPHET OF BERKELEY SQUARE

A PLAY IN FIVE ACTS

FRANK J. MORLOCK

Adapted from the Novel by Robert Hichens

THE BORGO PRESS
MMXIII

THE PROPHET OF BERKELEY SQUARE

Copyright © 1987, 2013 by Frank J. Morlock

FIRST BORGO PRESS EDITION

Published by Wildside Press LLC

www.wildsidebooks.com

DEDICATION

To my friend, Tony Smith

CONTENTS

CAST OF CHARACTERS 9
ACT I, Scene 1 11
ACT I, Scene 2 23
ACT I, Scene 3 45
ACT II, Scene 4 61
ACT III, Scene 5 98
ACT III, Scene 6 104
ACT IV, Scene 7 125
ACT IV, Scene 8 140
ACT V, Scene 9 164
ABOUT THE AUTHOR 192

CAST OF CHARACTERS

Hennessey Vivian, would-be Prophet of Berkeley Square

Ferdinand, Hennessey's butler

Gustavus, Hennessey's footman

Mrs. Merillia, Hennessey's grandmother

Fancy, Mrs. Merillia's maid

Jupiter Malkiel II, aka Sagittarius

Lady Enid, aka Miss Minerva

Sir Tiglath Butt, astronomer

Librarian, employee at Jellybrand's

Mrs. Sophronia Malkiel, wife of Malkiel the Second

Lady Julia Postlethwaite, dinner guest of Mrs. Merillia

Mrs. Bridgman, society hostess dabbling in the occult

Mr. Biggle, clergyman, guest at Mrs. Bridgman's party

Footman at Mrs. Bridgman's party

Mr. Briskin, party guest

Eureka, medium

Harriet, party guest

Mr. Amos Towle, medium

Other party guests

Bobby, policeman

ACT I
SCENE 1

The action takes place in London circa 1900.

A room in Hennessey Vivian's mansion, Berkeley Square.

Hennessey (speaking to the butler with considerable agitation)

Has Mr. Malkiel sent any reply to my inquiry?

Ferdinand

He has not, sir.

Hennessey

Did the messenger say he delivered my note?

Ferdinand

He said so, sir, on his Bible oath.

Hennessey

And, do you believe him?

Ferdinand

Oh, sir! Surely, a London boy would not be found to tell a lie.

Hennessey

I hope not, Ferdinand. Still—did he look a nervous sort?

Ferdinand

He was a trifle pale about the gill—but a heart of gold, I feel sure.

Hennessey

Nevertheless, he may have been frightened to go to Mr. Malkiel's door. That will do. (changing his mind) Wait! Mrs. Merillia has gone to the Gaiety Theatre tonight. I expect her back soon. She may need assistance on her return.

Ferdinand

Assistance, sir? Mrs. Merillia, sir?

Hennessey

She may—I say—she may—have to be carried to bed.

Ferdinand

I'll have an armchair ready, sir.

Hennessey

Mrs. Merillia must not be dropped.

Ferdinand (calling to a footman)

Gustavus, Mrs. Merillia will be back soon. She may need assistance on her return, Gustavus.

Gustavus (entering)

Assistance, Mr. Ferdinand! Mrs. Merillia, Mr. Ferdinand!

Ferdinand

She may—we say—she may—have to be carried to bed, Gustavus.

Gustavus

I'll have an armchair ready, Mr. Ferdinand.

Ferdinand

Mrs. Merillia must not be dropped, Gustavus.

Mrs. Merillia's Voice

Help!

(The three men rush out.)

All nonsense, Hennessey, all rubbish! There's not much wrong with me, is there?

(Enter Mrs. Merillia, a still fashionable woman in her mid-fifties, carried by Gustavus and awkwardly assisted by Ferdinand and Hennessey.)

Hennessey

Dearest Grannie—

Mrs. Merillia

You shouldn't have prophesized, and I shouldn't have jumped.

Hennessey

Is it—?

Mrs. Merillia

Sprained? I'm afraid so. Hoist me over there. Set me down by the fire.—And now, bring me a sandwich, a brandy and water, too, if you please. Yes, put the footstool well under me.

(Exit Ferdinand.)

Hennessey

Dearest Grannie—are you in great pain?

Mrs. Merillia

No, Hennessey. Are you?

Hennessey

I?

Mrs. Merillia

Yes, at my accident. Tell me, are you really pained that I have had the accident you prophesied?

Hennessey

I am sincerely grieved, I am indeed.

Mrs. Merillia

And, if I had not hurt myself, would you still have been sincerely grieved?

Hennessey

I hope not, Grannie.

Mrs. Merillia

Most people would. Why be singular? You see, this prophetic business has made you pleased over my accident.

Hennessey

No, no, that's impossible. It cannot be.

Mrs. Merillia

If I had failed to have an accident tonight, you'd have been mad at the stars: Mercury, Uranus, Jupiter, Saturn, and Venus.

Hennessey

I confess it is true.

Mrs. Merillia

Exactly. Prophecy is dangerous. If you hadn't predicted

I'd have an accident, I would never have run upstairs to prove you wrong.

Hennessey

But, Grannie, I assure you, I as most anxious to save you. I hoped I had made a mistake. I even sent to Mr. Malkiel.

Mrs. Merillia

Mr. Malkiel? Who is he? Do we know him?

Hennessey

No. But he has written a marvelous *Almanac*.

Mrs. Merillia

Surely, it's not one man?

Hennessey

So I thought, but I've found out he really is just one person. He's a very retiring and secretive fellow. But I've discovered that he receives and answers letter inquiries at an address in London.

Mrs. Merillia

Indeed. Where is it?

Hennessey

Jellybrand's Library. I sent a messenger there today.

Mrs. Merillia

Did you receive a reply?

Hennessey

No. I think the messenger bolted. In any case, I got no answer. How are you feeling?

Mrs. Merillia

Twisted, but prophetic. I foretell my ankle will be swelled beyond recognition tomorrow.

Hennessey

Oh, Grannie, how can you joke—?

Mrs. Merillia

Hennessey, you are grown to look like Lord Broudling, when he combined the Premiership with the Foreign Office and we had that dreadful complication with Ireland. My dear boy, you are corrupted with thought and care. Has Venus been playing you another jade's trick?

Hennessey

I have scarcely looked at Venus since—since I became a prophet, Grannie. I have scarcely dared to.

Mrs. Merillia

I'm glad to hear it. Venus always has a dangerous influence on impressionable young men. If you want to look at anybody, look at Lady Enid. Now, she is sensible.

Hennessey

Yes, Lady Enid is sensible, Grannie.—I think it my duty to see Mr. Malkiel.

Mrs. Merillia

The *Almanac* man? Whatever do you want with him?

Hennessey

To learn his views on this strange faculty of prophecy. Among all our immense acquaintance, we don't number a single prophet.

Mrs. Merillia

One can't know everybody. And, I believe that prophets always spring from the lowest classes. The line must be drawn somewhere, even in these days.

Hennessey

Why not draw it at millionaires then?

Mrs. Merillia

I should like nothing better. Something will have to be done. If nobodies go everywhere, then somebodies will soon go nowhere.

Hennessey

Perhaps, they do go nowhere. Prophets have always been inclined to dwell in the wilderness.

Mrs. Merillia

But, where can you find a wilderness these days? What sort of person do you expect this Malkiel to be?

Hennessey

Something quite out of the ordinary, quite out of the common.

(Enter Ferdinand and Fancy with sandwiches, etc.,)

Ferdinand

Your sandwiches, ma'am.

Mrs. Merillia

That's all right. Bring it along, and help me to bed.

(Exit Mrs. Merillia, Gustavus, and Ferdinand.)

Hennessey

Goodnight, Grannie.

Fancy

Goodnight, ma'am.

Hennessey

Fancy, you know me well.

Fancy

From the bottle, sir.

Hennessey

Fancy, have you ever thought—?

Fancy

I can't say I have, sir.

Hennessey

Fancy, if a man finds out he is a prophet, what ought

he to do?

Fancy

Let it alone, sir. Let it alone, Master Hennessey.

Hennessey

What do you mean by that?

Fancy

What I say, sir.

Hennessey

But, can't you explain, Fancy?

Fancy

Oh, Master Hennessey, the lives that have been wrecked, the homes that have been broken up by explainings.

CURTAIN

ACT I
SCENE 2

Jellybrand's Library.

Malkiel and Hennessey enter.

Malkiel

And now, sir—now, sir, what do you want with me?

Hennessey

Malkiel the Second, I wish to speak to you as one prophet to another.

Malkiel

Do you live in Berkeley Square, sir, and claim to be a prophet?

Hennessey

I do.

Malkiel

The assumption seems rather ridiculous—forgive me! The Berkeley Square! Whatever will Madame say?

Hennessey

Madame?

Malkiel

Madame Malkiel.

Hennessey

Your wife?

Malkiel

My honored lady.—But what can you know of prophecy in such a fashionable neighborhood?

Hennessey

What influence can neighborhood have on such a super terrestrial matter?

Malkiel

Did Isiah reside in Berkeley Square, sir?

Hennessey

I fancy not, still—

Malkiel

I fancy not, too. Nor any prophet I ever heard of. No, no, sir, Madame is quite right. She married me, despite the damning, yes, I say, sir, the damning fact that I was a prophet—but she made me take a solemn oath.

Hennessey

What was it?

Malkiel

What was it, do you say?

Hennessey

Yes, I do, sir.

Malkiel

It was this, sir. To mix with no prophets so long as we both should live. Prophets, she said are low class, dirty persons. Their influence would be bad for the children when they begin to grow up. How could Corona make her debut in prophetic circles? How could she do it, sir?

Hennessey (helplessly)

I don't know, I'm sure.

Malkiel

Nor I, sir, nor I. And, it's the same with Capricornus. My boy shall not be thrown in with prophets. Did Malkiel the First start the *Almanac* for that? Did he, I say?

Hennessey

I haven't an idea.

Malkiel

He did not, sir. And did I? No, sir. Am I dressed like a prophet?

Hennessey

No, certainly not.

Malkiel

Do I bear myself prophetically?

Hennessey

Certainly not.

Malkiel (triumphantly)

No. I might have been anybody. Other prophets there are, but there is only one Malkiel. Wait a few years, sir, only wait.

Hennessey

Certainly, I will.

Malkiel

Wait till the children grow up. Then, and only then, will you know if Malkiel the Second is the exception to the rule of prophets.

Hennessey

I will, sir.

Malkiel

And now, I am at your service, sir. I am all attention.

Hennessey

I want to consult you about my strange powers.

Malkiel

Strange powers in Berkeley Square? But, go on sir. What are they?

Hennessey

Having studied the stars, I made a prophecy.

Malkiel

Weather forecast, I suppose. The easiest kind, sir. Beginner's stuff. But, go on, sir, go on.

Hennessey

If that had been all, I daresay I should have thought very little of the matter.

Malkiel

Nonsense, sir! Who thinks their first baby a little one? Can you tell me that?

Hennessey

Perhaps you're right.

Malkiel

Well, sir, what of your second attempt? In the Berkeley Square?

Hennessey

Malkiel the Second, in the Berkeley Square, I have a relation, an honored grandmother.

Malkiel

You've the better of me, then, sir. My parents and the Madame's are all in Brompton Cemetery. Well, sir, you've got an honored grandmother in Berkeley Square. What of it?

Hennessey

She is naturally elderly.

Malkiel

And you predicted her death and she passed over. Very natural, too, sir. The number two beginner's prophecy.

Hennessey

She did nothing of the kind.

Malkiel

You prophesied it, and she didn't pass over. Very natural, too, sir. I understand how you feel. Terrible when a prophecy goes wrong.

Hennessey

You are utterly mistaken.

Malkiel

In that case, I say no more. Proceed, sir. You cast your honored grandmother's horoscope—in the Berkeley Square?

Hennessey

I did, and I discovered she was going to have an accident.

Malkiel

Did she have it in the Square, sir?

Hennessey (defensively)

And, what if she did?

Malkiel

Point of information.

Hennessey

The accident did take place in the Square, and on the very night which I predicted.

Malkiel (pondering, upset)

Can Madame be wrong? Can Madame be wrong—all these many years?

Hennessey

What about?

Malkiel

Can it be, that a prophet should live in Berkeley Square? This matter must be thrashed out thoroughly. Sir, you may be a prophet, but if you are, you have proved myself sacrifice—my martyrdom—totally and entirely unnecessary. I will go further, sir, and I will say more. You have also proved the sacred intuition of a woman, a respectable, married woman—false and deceived. Remember this, sir, remember all this, then search yourself thoroughly, and say whether what you have told me is strictly true.

Hennessey

I assure you.

Malkiel

Search yourself, sir!

Hennessey

But, upon my honor—

Malkiel

Hush, sir, hush. I insist, that you search yourself thoroughly before you answer this momentous question.

Hennessey

I assure you, on my honor, that all I have said is strictly true.

Malkiel

And, took place in the Berkeley Square?

Hennessey

And, took place in the Berkeley Square.

Malkiel

It may have been chance. Beginner's luck. Still, it looks bad—very bad.

Hennessey

Explain yourself, Malkiel the Second. Why should my strange gift affect you?

Malkiel (suspiciously)

If you have it, sir.

Hennessey

Assuming I do, how does that affect you?

Malkiel

You desire my revelation, sir? You desire to enter into the bosom of a family that has hitherto dwelt apart?

Hennessey

I would not, for the world, intrude upon—

Malkiel

Well, perhaps you have the right. Jellybrand's has betrayed me to you. You know my name, my profession. Why should you not know more? Perhaps, it is better so! Malkiel the First who founded the *Almanac* was a great man—

Hennessey

I am sure he was—

Malkiel

Lived a retired life. He could not live like other men. He could not live in the Berkeley Square.

Hennessey

But—

Malkiel

At least, I thought so then, and have done so till today. So my father believed, and so Madame. We resolved to live a retired life so that it could suitably influence the minds of our children. For we resolved, sir, that with me, the *Almanac* should cease.—We all have our ambitions, and that was mine.

Hennessey

Good heavens! Malkiel's *Almanac* cease! But, why? Such a very useful institution.

Malkiel

Useful! There's nothing like it.

Hennessey

Then, why let it cease?

Malkiel

Because the social status of the prophet, sir, is not agreeable to myself or Madame.

Hennessey

Then, your Capricorn—er, your son, will not carry on?

Malkiel

Capricornus, a prophet, sir? Not if Madame and I know it. Capricornus is to be an architect. What do you say to that?

Hennessey

Is it really a better profession?

Malkiel

It is more select. Madame will not mix with prophets, but she has a very pleasant and select little circle.

Hennessey

Indeed.

Malkiel

Yes, sir. Architects and their wives.

Hennessey

Quite, quite.

Malkiel

They do not know who we are, sir. Except to you and Jellybrand's, we are the Sagittariuses of Sagittarius Lodge—living on a competence by the River Mouse.

They do not see the telescope—

Hennessey

Of course—

Malkiel (passionately)

For the children's sake.

Hennessey

Certainly, certainly.

Malkiel

And now, after all these years, YOU (accusingly) come to me and say, upon oath, that a prophet need not live in seclusion, but may live in—in Berkeley Square! (weeping) Of what use are the sacrifices of myself and Madame?

Hennessey

Malkiel the Second, be brave! You must see this thing through.

Malkiel

I know it, sir, I know it. And now, to business.

Hennessey

What business?

Malkiel

Mine. Mine, sir, and yours. You have chosen to enter my life. That act has given me the right to enter yours.

Hennessey (dubiously)

Is that so?

Malkiel (relentlessly)

This duty I shall carry out unflinchingly. At whatever cost to myself or you. This will not be our last interview. Do not think it.

Hennessey (desperately)

I assure you, I do not wish to think it.

Malkiel

It matters little whether you wish to do so or not. The son of Malkiel the First is not a man to be trifled with. From this day forth, you will be bound up with the *Almanac*.

Hennessey

Bound up? Merciful heavens.

Malkiel

For, why should it ever cease if a prophet can live openly in Berkeley Square? And now, sir, you must take a solemn pledge.—Till the last day—

Hennessey

What day?

Malkiel

Till the last, sir, you will reveal, to no living person, that there is such an individual as Malkiel.—That you have ever met him—who he is, or who Madame and family are. Unless I give the word. You owe me this. Swear!

Hennessey (relieved)

I swear.

Malkiel

I have your card, sir, here is mine. I shall confer at once with Madame. You will hear from me.

(Enter Lady Enid at the back.)

Malkiel (startled)

Miss Minerva!

Hennessey (unnerved)

Lady Enid!

(Lady Enid, seeing Hennessey and Malkiel, retreats quickly and exits to another room. Enter Sir Tiglath, an apoplectic old astronomer followed by a protesting Librarian.)

Tiglath

Bandy no words with me, infamous malapert! Answer my question! Have you a young female concealed within these loathsome precincts?

Librarian

Loathsome precincts, yourself! You're a nice one, you are, chasing respectable ladies about at your age! There ain't no young females in the library, and if there was, I shouldn't trot 'em out for you to clap your eyes on. Now then, out yer go. No more words about it. Out yer go.

(The Librarian pushes Tiglath off. There are sounds of a struggle.)

Malkiel

I must not be seen. But remember, sir, I shall probe you, probe you to the core.

(Malkiel exits. Enter Lady Enid and the Librarian.)

Librarian

You must need a glass of wine, Miss Minerva?

Enid

Thank you. (drinking) I'm poisoned.

Hennessey

What is it, Lady Enid?

Librarian

What, by the old gent?

Enid

By that wine. Get me a glass of water—a glass of water!

Librarian

It's all right, ma'am. The old gentleman's gone.

Enid

What old gentleman? Give me a glass of water, or I shall die.

Hennessey

Where'd you get this wine?

Librarian

From next to the rabbit shop across the street. Maybe you need a doctor?

Enid

Take me to one.

Librarian

There's one on the other side of the rabbit shop.

Enid

It's all right. I feel much better now.

Librarian

I'm sorry, I don't have any water. Water abut here is no good. That's why I keep wine.

Enid

It's all right, it's all right.

Librarian

If the lady is better, I will trust her to you. Imagine the nerve of the old geezer? Following a respectable lady right off the street. Now I must get back to my desk.

(Exit Librarian.)

Enid

What a strange person. (silence) It's nice of you not to ask any questions, Mr. Vivian.

Hennessey

Hennessey, Lady Enid, Hennessey.

Enid

I'm a woman, and I don't know if I can be so nice.

Hennessey

Try—please.

Enid

I have tried, but I cannot succeed. Why on earth were

you meeting with Mr. Sagittarius?

Hennessey

Then, Lady Enid—YOU are really Miss Minerva Partridge?

Enid

Now, we're neither of us nice. But, we're both human. Well?

Hennessey

I'm sorry, I can't tell you.

Enid (annoyed)

Oh, all right. But now, I'm at a disadvantage. You know I'm Miss Minerva.

Hennessey

Yes, but I don't know why you are, or who the old gentleman was.—Why not come to tea with Grannie?

Enid (surprised)

She's at home! She must have twisted her ankle.

Hennessey

Yes, she did.

Enid

Then, then, I think I shall.

CURTAIN

ACT I
SCENE 3

A room in Hennessey Vivian's mansion. Same as Scene 1. Mrs. Merillia and Sir Tiglath are having tea.

Enter Hennessey and Lady Enid.

Hennessey

Sir Tiglath! This is indeed a pleasure.

Tiglath (startled, choking on his muffin)

Only a Persian could devour this muffin now. Omar, beneath his tree, perhaps. Wherefore do you startle hapless guests, young man, and cause the poor astronomer to cast his muffin into the potpourri?

Enid (bravely)

How'd you do, Sir Tiglath?

Tiglath

Very ill, very ill. One has had an afternoon of tragedy,

an afternoon of brawling and of disturbance in a place that shall henceforth be called accursed. Thrice accursed.

Hennessey (offering roses to Mrs. Merillia)

These are a little late, Grannie, but I was unavoidably detained.

Mrs. Merillia

Detained, Hennessey? Then, you found what you were seeking?

Hennessey

No, no, Grannie. I met Lady Enid.

Tiglath

Where did you meet the lady, young man? Was it in that accursed place?

Hennessey (innocently)

What place is that, Sir Tiglath?

Tiglath

The place of perfidy, young man, in which the defenders of foolish virgins are buffeted and browbeaten by monsters of indeterminate sex with craniums as big as the great nebula of Orion. Let dragons lay it waste like the Towers of Babylon.

Mrs. Merillia

I think Sir Tiglath must be describing Shaftesbury Avenue.

Hennessey

Really, I had no idea that it was such an evil neighborhood.

Enid (butter wouldn't melt in her mouth)

Where is Shaftesbury Avenue?

Tiglath

Where partridges are to be found in January.

Enid (seemingly perplexed)

What do you mean, Sir Tiglath? (to Mrs. Merillia, confidentially) He never talks sensibly unless he is in his observatory or lecturing the Royal Society on the "Regularity of the Heavenly Bodies."

Tiglath (darkly)

The irregularities of earthly ones.

Mrs. Merillia

I fear, Sir Tiglath, you must be a member of the Vigilance Society.

Enid

He observes the morals of the universe through his telescope. (to Hennessey) By the way, do you, too?

Hennessey

I confess that I watch the heavens through that window.

Tiglath (suspiciously)

And, for what purpose, young man?

Hennessey

For the purposes of research, Sir Tiglath.

Tiglath

The young man trieth to put off the old astronomer with fair words. The thief inserteth his thumb into the tail pocket of the unobservant archbishop to find out what's there. The young man playeth merrily forsooth with the old astronomer.

Hennessey

Grannie, you know how deeply the heavenly bodies interest me.

Tiglath

For their own sake, young man? Or as the accursed place interests foolish virgins—for the sake of frivolity, idle curiosity, or dark doings? Can you tell your admirable and revered grandam that?

Hennessey

I was originally led to the study of the stars, Sir Tiglath, because I had the honor to meet you and make your acquaintance.

Tiglath

In what fair company did the old astronomer converse with the young man? He doteth and cannot remember the occasion.

Hennessey

It was at the Colley Cibber Club, Sir Tiglath. But, we—we didn't converse. You had a—a slight indisposition.

Tiglath

Would you venture to imply, in the presence of your

notable grandam, that one had looked upon the wine when it was red, young man?

Hennessey

You had a glass of port by you, certainly. But you also had a cold—which—you gave me to understand by signs—had affected your throat and prevented you from carrying on a conversation.

Tiglath

Then, it was the vision of the old astronomer's personal and starry beauty that led you, hot foot, to Venus through yonder telescope?

Hennessey

I began an examination into the Milky Way.

Tiglath

Go on, young man, the old astronomer lendeth ear.

Hennessey (honestly)

I began to think of nothing else. I could talk of nothing else. Could I, Grannie?

Mrs. Merillia

All other topics were banished from discussion.

Hennessey

All. I could not bear to tear myself from the telescope. I longed for a perpetual night, and found the day intolerably irksome.

Tiglath

The old astronomer approveth the young man's admiration for the heavenly bodies. Go on.

Hennessey

That's all, Sir Tiglath.

Tiglath (wrathfully)

Sir, are you a man of science, or have you the brain of a charlatan enclosed in the filthy fleshy envelope of a conjuror?

Hennessey

I—

Tiglath

Do you study the noble and beautiful stars for their own sakes—or do you peek and pry at them through the keyhole of a contemptible curiosity to discover what they can do for you?

Hennessey

I—

Tiglath

Which are you, sir, a young man of parts, or an insulter of the heavens, a Peeping Tom of the Universe?

Hennessey

I—

Tiglath

What do you ask the stars, sir? Tell the old astronomer that?

Hennessey

What do I ask, Sir Tiglath?

Tiglath

Do you afflict the heavens with ridiculous inquiries? Is that it?

Mrs. Merillia

Yes, Hennessey, I have thought it for the best. At my age, I am not equal to living at close quarters with a determined young prophet, so Sir Tiglath knows all about it.

Enid

All about what?

Hennessey

Grannie means that I—that I have been enabled by the stars to foretell certain future events.

Tiglath

Ohh!

Enid

What? Like Malkiel's *Almanac* does?

Hennessey

Don't! Don't, Sir Tiglath.

Mrs. Merillia

Oh, Sir Tiglath—don't!

Enid

No, no—please don't, Sir Tiglath.

Hennessey

For heaven's sake—don't!

Fancy

The gentleman's about to burst, ma'am.

Tiglath

Have you ever heard where liars go to, woman?

Mrs. Merillia

Yes, yes, it's all right, Fancy, it's all right. We all agree with you, Sir Tiglath. Now, now, you mustn't cry.

Enid

There, sit down and compose yourself.

Tiglath

The stars in their courses tremble when the accursed name of Malkiel is mentioned. The old astronomer is dissolved in wrath at the sound of the pernicious word.

Mrs. Merillia

There, Hennessey! You see what Sir Tiglath says.

Tiglath

If Malkiel were an individual instead of the name of a syndicate, the old astronomer, well stricken in years though he be, would HUNT HIM OUT OF HIS HIDING PLACE AND SLAY HIM WITH THESE FEEBLE AND SCIENTIFIC HANDS!

Mrs. Merillia

But, Malkiel is—

Enid

I thought Malkiel was a man.

Tiglath

He—for I will not foul my lips again with his accursed name—is not a man.

Mrs. Merillia

Pray, Sir Tiglath, don't—for with my sprained ankle, I am really not equal to it.

Hennessey

But, how can a syndicate turn itself into a prophet?

Tiglath

Young man, you talk idly. What are companies formed for, if not to make profits? Everyone is a company nowadays.

Enid

Well, but how are you sure that the *Almanac* person is also plural, Sir Tiglath?

Tiglath

Because, I sought him with the firm intention of killing him these five and forty years. I only gave up my Christian quest when I was assured on excellent authority that he was a company. May bulls and bears destroy him!

Enid

Well, that's very odd. Very odd, indeed. And I never guessed it.

Mrs. Merillia

Guessed what, my dear?

Enid

Why that Malkiel's a company.

Hennessey

Nor I.

Mrs. Merillia

Then, Hennessey, now you've heard Sir Tiglath's opinion, I'm sure you'll never study the stars again. Come, promise me! Sir Tiglath, join your voice to mine.

Tiglath

Young man, your revered grandam asks of you a righteous thing.

Hennessey

I—

Tiglath

Who are you to trifle with those shining worlds that make the beauty of the night and that stir eternity in the soul of man?

Hennessey

I—

Tiglath

Who are you to think those glittering monsters have

nothing to do but inform your pigmy brain of marriages, mishaps, deaths, and births?

Hennessey

I—

Tiglath

Who are you to knock at the gates of heaven and clamor to know the future? Answer me that?

Hennessey

Very well! I'll give it up.

Mrs. Merillia

Thank you, Sir Tiglath. I knew you would persuade the boy.

Tiglath

Let the morning stars, freed from insult—sing together.

Enid

I must go!

Tiglath

The old astronomer will protect the injudicious young

female—lest she wander forth into an accursed place.

Enid (snappishly)

I'm only going to Hill Street. (to Hennessey) Come and see me tomorrow. (low) We must have a talk. Don't tell anybody.

(Exit Lady Enid and Sir Tiglath. Enter Ferdinand.)

Hennessey

Mr. Ferdinand.

Ferdinand

Sir?

Hennessey

Kindly call Gustavus to your aid, and take away the telescope.

Ferdinand

Sir!

Hennessey

Take away the telescope.

Ferdinand

Where shall I place it, sir?

Hennessey

Anywhere. In the pantry, if you like.

Ferdinand

Very well, sir. In the pantry. It will be useful there.

CURTAIN

ACT II
SCENE 4

A room in Hennessey Vivian's mansion.

Enter Hennessey and Lady Enid.

Hennessey

Do sit down, dear Lady Enid.

Enid

I've guessed your secret, Mr. Vivian.

Hennessey (cannily)

Which one?

Enid (pouting)

Which? Oh, Mr. Vivian—and I thought you trusted me.

Hennessey

I'm sorry.

Enid

I always think that nearly all the miseries of the world come about from people not trusting in—in people.

Hennessey

Or, from trusting the wrong people. Which is it?

Enid

Why did you stop me from telling Sir Tiglath that Malkiel was a person, not a syndicate?

Hennessey

Did I stop you?

Enid

With your look.

Hennessey

Because, I was sure—certain you—couldn't be sure.

Enid

How could you be so certain?

Hennessey

How?

Enid

How?

Hennessey

Well, how is one certain of anything?

Enid

How are you certain that I'm Miss Minerva Partridge?

Hennessey

Because you told me so yourself. Because you came in Jellybrand's for your letters.

Enid

Haven't I seen Malkiel come to Jellybrand's for his letters?

Hennessey

Does he go to Jellybrand's? But, he's a company. Sir Tiglath said so.

Enid

And, what did your look say, yesterday?

Hennessey

I had a cold in my eyes yesterday.

Enid

Mr. Vivian, I am going to confide in you. I'm going to throw myself on your mercy. I'm going to trust you.

Hennessey (uneasily)

Many thanks. (aside) Dear, dear.

Enid

I dare say you know, Mr. Vivian, that people always call me a very sensible sort of girl.

Hennessey

I know they do.

Enid

What do they mean by that?

Hennessey

Mean? Why, I suppose they mean you're—er—

sensible.

Enid

I'm going to tell you what they mean. They mean a girl who likes fresh air, sports, and thinks the Daily Mail is an intellectual sort of paper. That's what they mean by a sensible sort of girl, (accusingly) isn't it?

Hennessey

I daresay it is. Aren't you?

Enid

No, I am not. I'm Miss Minerva Partridge.

Hennessey

Well, but what is that?

Enid

Why, it's my secret.

Hennessey

Oh—

Enid

Now, I can tell you, because I know you're silly, too.

Hennessey

Humph!

Enid

I've been Miss Minerva Partridge for—wait a moment, I must consult my diary. (fumbles in her purse and extracts diary) It's foolish to keep one, isn't it?

Hennessey (agreeably)

Very foolish, indeed.

Enid

I'm so glad you think so. Ah, exactly a year and a half.

Hennessey

So long as that?

Enid

Yes. A double life.

Hennessey

Many people do that. One meets people who lead double lives almost every day.

Enid

I can't say I do.

Hennessey

Please, go on. I am so interested. Why have you done it?

Enid

Mr. Vivian, many girls are born sensible looking. It isn't their fault.

Hennessey

Are they really? It never occurred to me.

Enid

They don't always wish it.

Hennessey

Fancy that.

Enid

Such things rarely occur to men.—You can understand that to be born sensible looking and not wishing it—is very trying.

Hennessey

What is?

Enid

To look sensible. It's something to do with the shape of my eyebrows.

Hennessey

ER—no doubt.

Enid

Mr. Vivian, I'll tell you now, that I've never been sensible in my entire life.

Hennessey (shocked)

Never?

Enid

Never. I have been in a perpetual condition of acting sensibly—quite against my will.

Hennessey

How very troublesome.

Enid

Nobody knows but you how I've suffered.

Hennessey

Why—do I know?

Enid

You know intuitively, because you're almost as silly as I am. I was furious with you when you told Sir Tiglath you'd give it up. You mustn't give it up.

Hennessey

You were furious with me?

Enid

Absolutely. I wanted to scratch your face.

Hennessey

This is astounding.

Enid

Were you leading a double life at Jellybrand's?

Hennessey (quickly)

Oh, no, not at all. I never do anything of the sort.

Enid

Sure!

Hennessey

Certainly not. Nothing could induce me.

Enid (crestfallen)

How disappointing.

Hennessey

But, why did you try to avoid Sir Tiglath?

Enid

Well, he's a very strange, peculiar old man.

Hennessey

Peculiar? Yes, he is.

Enid

Oh, not that. Lots of elderly men have purple faces and roaring voices. No, you see, he's old, but he's not the least bit silly.

Hennessey

He looks silly.

Enid

That's how he gets away with it. The opposite of me. No one suspects him of being sensible. It's strange, because folly improves with age.—Sir Tiglath is crazy about me.

Hennessey

Really! I can't say I blame him.

Enid

You think that proves he's silly, don't you?

Hennessey

Not at all, not at all.

(Enter Ferdinand discreetly.)

Ferdinand

Sir, the pair of persons you expected has come.

Hennessey

You haven't disturbed Mrs. Merillia with them, I hope?

Ferdinand

No, sir, indeed. I begged them to walk on tiptoe.

Hennessey

What?

Ferdinand

I informed them there was illness in the house.

Hennessey

And did they, er—?

Ferdinand

The male person got on his toes at once, but the female person shrieked out: "Is it catching? Think of Capericornopus!"—or something of that sort. I took the liberty to say ankles is not catching, and that I would think of Capericornopus if she would walk on tiptoe.

Hennessey

Bring some tea, Mr. Ferdinand—quietly—and if Mrs. Merillia should ask for me—say I'm writing.

Ferdinand

Master Hennessey, I am a London butler, and you ask me to—!

Hennessey

Say, I'm busy—that will be quite true. I shall be very busy.

(Exit Ferdinand.)

Enid (rising)

I really must go. I will leave you to your guests.

Hennessey

Let me escort you to the door, Lady Enid.

(Exit Lady Enid and Hennessey. After a moment, enter Mrs. and Mr. Malkiel [Sagittarius].)

Mrs. Malkiel

How are we to know it's only ankles?

Malkiel (protesting)

But, the gentleman who opened the door said—

Mrs. Malkiel

You are over fifty years of age, and you still trust a London butler?

Malkiel

I cannot help it. Indeed, I can't, Sophronia. I am as I am.

Mrs. Malkiel

Did Shakespeare imply that when he invented his immortal Valpone? Did Carlyle—

Malkiel (placatingly)

Perhaps not, my dear. You know best. Still, ordinary men—not that I claim to be an ordinary man—but ordinary men must remain to a certain extent what they are.

Mrs. Malkiel

Then, of what use was Plato to the Republic?

(Enter Ferdinand and Hennessey.)

Ferdinand

Shall I set the tea on the mat, sir?

Hennessey

I really must apologize for being late. (to Ferdinand, indicating the tea) Over there.

Malkiel

I thought I said "sharp," sir.

Hennessey

Wasn't I sharp? Will you please present me?

Malkiel (to his wife)

Are you equal to it, my love? (his wife nods) Madame Sagittarius, sir, my wife, the mother of Corona and Capricornus.

Hennessey

I thought you might like to have some tea.

Mrs. Malkiel

Thank you. It would be acceptable. The long journey from the banks of the Mouse to these central districts is not without its fatigue. A beautiful equipage.

Hennessey

You've seen the brougham?

Mrs. Malkiel

What broom?

Hennessey

I thought—

Mrs. Malkiel (icily)

The tea equipage.

Hennessey

Oh, yes. Queen Anne Silver.

Mrs. Malkiel

A great woman! A noble creature. A pity she died.

Hennessey

A great pity, indeed.

Mrs. Malkiel

Still—it was the will of Providence. Reflect on that.

Hennessey

Quite so.

(Mr. Ferdinand leaves after having served the tea.)

Mrs. Malkiel

As the mother of Corona and Capricornus, I felt it my

duty to ask you, Mr.—

Hennessey

Vivian.

Mrs. Malkiel

Mr. Vivian, whether it is only ankles, as the gentleman who opened the door assured me.

Hennessey

It is only that.

Mrs. Malkiel

Not catching?

Hennessey

Oh, dear, no.

Malkiel

There, Sophronia, I told you it was merely prophecy.— And now, sir, now that we are alone—

Mrs. Malkiel

Kindly permit our host to succor my fatigue.

Hennessey

I think I ought to tell you at once, that there is no need for further anxiety. I have put down my telescope. I've come to the conclusion that I overrated my powers as amateurs sometimes do. I think I shall take up golf instead.

Mrs. Malkiel

Indeed!

Malkiel

That won't do, sir, at this time of day. That won't do at all—will it, Madame?

Mrs. Malkiel

You should have thought of that yesterday.

Malkiel

You hear her, sir, you grasp her meaning?

Hennessey

Certainly, I hear her.

Malkiel

Madame is a lady of deep learning. There can be no

going back, sir—can there, Madame?

Mrs. Malkiel

No human creature can go back. Such is the law of nature discovered by Darwin in his Origin of the Species. No human creature can go back. Least of all this gentleman. He must go forward, and we with him.

Hennessey

But—

Mrs. Malkiel

There is no such word as "but" in my dictionary.

Hennessey

An abridged edition, no doubt.

Mrs. Malkiel

I am better now, Jupiter. If you are ready, we can explain the test to the gentleman.

Hennessey

No test will be necessary. My telescope has already been removed to the pantry.

Mrs. Malkiel

Then it must be reinstated, sir, and this very night.

Malkiel

Madame has hit upon a plan, sir, for searching you to the quick. Trust a woman for that!

Hennessey

I shall naturally trust Madame Malkiel.

Mrs. Malkiel

So you say, sir. Our business is to find out whether, living in Berkeley Square, you can bring off a prophecy; or not.

Malkiel

Le me see, my dear, what was it to be?

Mrs. Malkiel

The honored grandmother one.

Hennessey

I can't possibly consent.

Mrs. Malkiel

Pray, Mr. Vivian, attend to me.

Malkiel

Pray, sir, attend to Madame.

Hennessey

But, I must, really—

Mrs. Malkiel

January is a month of grave importance to grandmothers this year.

Malkiel

Yes, my dear. The crab will be very busy till the third of February.

Hennessey

Quite.

Mrs. Malkiel

At which date, the little dog assumes his role of maleficent towards the aged.

Malkiel

When was the old lady born, if you please?

Hennessey

What old lady?

Mrs. Malkiel

The old lady who's got ankles—your honored grandmother?

Hennessey

On the twentieth of this month, but—

Mrs. Malkiel

At what time?

Hennessey

Six in the morning.

Mrs. Malkiel

Under what star?

Hennessey

Saturn, but—

Mrs. Malkiel

That's lucky. That brings her into touch with the Camelopard.

Malkiel (significantly)

Into very close touch.

Hennessey

I cannot conceivably permit—

Mrs. Malkiel

Will the Scorpion be round on her birthday?

Malkiel

Close round, my love. With the Serpent.

Mrs. Malkiel

You know the effect they'll have on her, don't you?

Malkiel

I should rather think so, my darling.

Mrs. Malkiel

And now, Mr. Vivian, I shall have to lay down the procedures that you will follow. I will direct you. Let's see—what's today?

Malkiel

The seventeenth, my love.

Mrs. Malkiel

Very well, today, being the seventeenth, and the old lady's birthday being the twentieth, you have three nights of steady work before you.

Hennessey (gloomily)

Steady work.

Mrs. Malkiel

What shall be his hours? Shall I say nine?

Malkiel

Nine would be too early. Eleven p.m. would be more to the purpose.

Mrs. Malkiel

Eleven let it be, then. And, how long shall his hours run? Eleven to dawn, I suppose?

Malkiel

Eleven to three should be sufficient.

Mrs. Malkiel

Oh, ver well—till three, then.

(Enter Ferdinand.)

Ferdinand

If you please, sir, I was to tell you that Lady Enid is taking tea with your grandmother. Mrs. Merillia thought you would like to know.

(Exit Ferdinand.)

Hennessey (delighted, to Malkiel)

I regret, more than I can say, that I shall be obliged to obey my grandmother's summons.—Suppose we defer?

Mrs. Malkiel

Impossible, sir! You must begin your work tonight, and how can you do it without your directions?

Hennessey

Oh, I can manage all right.

Mrs. Malkiel

The road from Berkeley Square to the stars is not so easy.

Hennessey

Then, kindly give me your directions as briefly as possible.

Mrs. Malkiel

Swear to follow them?

Hennessey

Yes, yes. Anything, anything.

Mrs. Malkiel

You have a star map?

Hennessey

No.

Mrs. Malkiel

Then, get one.

Hennessey

Very well.

Mrs. Malkiel

Very well. Having done so, and keeping the old lady perpetually in your mind, you will place her in the claws of the crab.

Hennessey (horrified)

What?

Malkiel

Mentally, sir, mentally.

Hennessey (relieved)

Oh.

Mrs. Malkiel

And, allowing for the natural effects of the Scorpion and the Serpent—

Hennessey (again horrified)

Good heavens!

Mrs. Malkiel

—when close round her, as they will be—But you will observe that for yourself. You will trace the cycloidal curve of the planets. Can you do that?—Good. Should the Lynx be near—

Hennessey (protesting)

No, no, it shall not be near!

Mrs. Malkiel

Well, you shall have to watch out for it. But, should it be, you will commit to paper what result its presence is likely to produce, and inform me by post on—what day?

Malkiel

Thursday morning.

Mrs. Malkiel

Is that quite—

Malkiel

Oh, quite, quite.

Mrs. Malkiel

With full particulars.

Hennessey

Full particulars? What of?

Malkiel

Of her weaning, cutting her first tooth, first period, date of marriage, widowhood, rashes—

Mrs. Malkiel

Especially the rashes.

Malkiel (wonderingly)

What a mind!

(Enter Ferdinand.)

Ferdinand

Her Ladyship says she really must go.

Hennessey

I must go. You see how I am circumstanced.

Mrs. Malkiel

You swear, sir, to carry out all our directions?

Hennessey

I do. Let me show you out—

(Enter Lady Enid.)

Enid

Why, Hennessey, I really thought—

Malkiel

Why, it's Miss Minerva.

Hennessey

This way, this way.

Malkiel

Then, she leads a double life, too.

Mrs. Malkiel

She? Who?

Malkiel

All of us, my love, all of us.

Hennessey

Goodbye.

Mrs. Malkiel

First post, Thursday.

(The Malkiels exit.)

Hennessey

Mr. Ferdinand, what has become of the telescope?

Ferdinand

I have removed it, sir, according to your order.

Hennessey

Where have you placed it?

Ferdinand

Well, sir, you said I might place it in Piccadilly, if I chose.

Hennessey

I see. You have done so?

Ferdinand

Well, no, sir.

Hennessey

Then, where is it?

Ferdinand

Well, for the moment, I have set it in the butler's quarters.

Hennessey

Indeed.

Ferdinand

I thought it might be of use there.

Hennessey

Quite so, quite so.

Ferdinand

Shall I bring it back, sir?

Hennessey (recoiling)

Certainly not.

Ferdinand (going)

Sir.

Hennessey

One moment, Mr. Ferdinand.

Ferdinand (stopping)

Sir?

Hennessey

At what time to you generally go to bed when you don't sit up?

Ferdinand (puzzled)

Sometimes at one time, sir, and sometimes at another.

Hennessey

What is your usual hour for being—quite—entirely in bed?

Ferdinand

Entirely in bed, sir?

Hennessey

Yes, not partially in bed, but really and truly in bed?

Ferdinand

Well, when I am in bed, sir, I am.

Hennessey

And, when's that?

Ferdinand

By twelve, sir.

Hennessey

I thought as much. You sit up too late, Mr. Ferdinand.

Ferdinand (uneasily)

I hope sir, that I—

Hennessey

That's what makes you so pale and delicate.

Ferdinand (astounded)

Delicate, sir?

Hennessey

Yes. You should be in bed—thoroughly in bed—by ten-thirty, quarter to eleven at the latest. And Gustavus, too. I speak for your health's sake, believe me.

Ferdinand

Yes, sir. (going)

Hennessey

One moment, Mr. Ferdinand. As a London butler, I expect you to know many things.

Ferdinand

Many things, sir?

Hennessey

What, exactly, in your opinion, is the meaning of the term "honor"?

Ferdinand (helplessly)

Oh, it means many things, sir, don't you know?

Hennessey

I don't. In what direction does honor lie?

Ferdinand

I never thought of it having direction, sir.

Hennessey

Would an honorable man feel bound to keep a promise?

Ferdinand

Without a doubt, sir.

Hennessey

Hmm! But, would he feel bound to keep two promises?

Ferdinand

If he made them.

Hennessey

Suppose he had!

Ferdinand

Then, he would.

Hennessey

But, suppose those two promises were incompatible?

Ferdinand

Oh, dear.

Hennessey

Well, what do you think?

Ferdinand

That he was a damned fool, sir.

Hennessey (blushing)

Putting that aside, what would you advise him to do?

Ferdinand

Not to be such a fool again.

Hennessey

No, no—which promise ought he to keep?

Ferdinand (after a moment)

That's a stumper, sir.

CURTAIN

ACT III
SCENE 5

A room in Hennessey Vivian's Mansion. Same as Act II.

Hennessey

Grannie, you would tell me anything, wouldn't you?

Mrs. Merillia

Why, of course, my dear boy. But, what about?

Hennessey

About—about yourself.

Mrs. Merillia (taken aback)

There is nothing to hide, Hennessey. You know that.

Hennessey

I do. I do. Yours has been the best, the sweetest life the world has ever known.

Mrs. Merillia

Well—I don't wish to imply I've been a saint—

Hennessey

But, I do, Grannie.

Mrs. Merillia (cagily)

Now, what exactly do you want to know, Hennessey?

Hennessey

I have some, er—questions.

Mrs. Merillia

All right. Fire away.

Hennessey

The first is—when were you removed from the bottle?

Mrs. Merillia (indignantly)

The bottle, Hennessey! Never, never—how could you suppose—?

Hennessey

Answered, darling Grannie, answered!—And now—your first tooth?

Mrs. Merillia

My first what?

Hennessey

Tooth, when did you cut it?

Mrs. Merillia

I have no idea.

Hennessey

Did you ever wear a short coat?

Mrs. Merillia

I'm not a man.

Hennessey

Always a skirt?

Mrs. Merillia

Of course! Why—

Hennessey (with relief)

That's four.

Mrs. Merillia

Four what?

Hennessey

When did you put your hair up?

Mrs. Merillia

My hair up? I've always had a maid. Never.

Hennessey

Never. (writing) You were married very young?

Mrs. Merillia

Seventeen.

Hennessey

That's six.

Mrs. Merillia

Six what?

Hennessey

And now, Grannie, rashes?

Mrs. Merillia

Rashers?

Hennessey

No—rashes, Have you ever had any redness?

Mrs. Merillia

Certainly not.

Hennessey

And, now the most delicate—when did you first?

Mrs. Merillia

First what?

Hennessey

Er—first—first—you know.

Mrs. Merillia

What?

Hennessey

Er. (eagerly) Thank you, Grannie. I knew you never did, anyway.

Mrs. Merillia

Hennessey, you'd better see a doctor, really.

BLACKOUT

ACT III
SCENE 6

Darkness. Repeated sounds of knocking, and voices saying "Telegram." The lights go up. Hennessey and Mr. Ferdinand are in urgent discussion.

Hennessey

Assure the Lord Chancellor that the last telegram boy has been and gone—gone away, that is, Mr. Ferdinand, and that I pledge my sacred word, as a gentleman and as his neighbor, that I will not have another telegram today.

Ferdinand

Yes, sir. His Lordship desired that you should be informed that, according to the law regulating public abominations and intolerable street noises, you were—

Hennessey

Yes, yes, I know. Go tell his Lordship, and swear—

Ferdinand

I couldn't do that so soon again, sir, really.

Hennessey

Asseverate to his Lordship that the very last boy had knocked for the very last time.

Ferdinand

It wasn't so much the knocking, sir, his Lordship complained of, as the boys blocking the pavement.

Hennessey

Yes, yes—go at once.

Ferdinand (going)

Yes, sir.

Hennessey

Wait. Fix a bulletin to the door. "Owner of this house seriously ill. Pray do not knock or death will certainly ensue."

Ferdinand

Yes, sir.

(Exit Ferdinand.)

Hennessey

Now, Grannie will have some peace.

(Enter Mrs. Merillia on crutches.)

Mrs. Merillia

How many more telegrams to you expect, Hennessey? You have had twenty-seven in the last three hours.

Hennessey

Grannie, Grannie, forgive me; I assure you—

Mrs. Merillia

Don't be afraid to tell me, Hennessey. It is much better to know the worst and face it bravely.

Hennessey

Grannie, there will be no more. Nothing—not wild horses even—shall induce me.

Mrs. Merillia

Horses! Then, they are racing tips?

(Ferdinand enters with a telegram which he gives to

Mrs. Merillia who reads it aloud.)

Mrs. Merillia

"Shocked to hear you are so ill that a knock will kill you. Earnest sympathy!" Lord Piltlochy.—Ah, how things get about! Tell him the knocks have nearly killed us all, but we are bearing up as well as we can.

Ferdinand (exiting)

Yes, ma'am.

Mrs. Merillia

It is two o'clock now, Hennessey. At the present rate, you can expect about ninety more telegrams today.

(Ender Ferdinand.)

Ferdinand

Mrs. Hendrick Marshall has called, ma'am. She desired me to say she was horrified you was so near the point.

Mrs. Merillia

What point?

Ferdinand

The point of death. She had no idea at all, ma'am.

Mrs. Merillia

Thank Mrs. Hendrick Marshall, and say we shall try to keep from the point for the present.

Ferdinand (exiting)

Yes, ma'am.

Mrs. Merillia

The numbers go up as the afternoon goes on, Hennessey.

Hennessey

Grannie, haven't I sworn—?

(Enter Ferdinand.)

Ferdinand

The Chancellor of the Exchequer, ma'am, desires his compliments. He had no conception you was dying, and he desires you to last out if possible till he has fetched Sir William Broadbent to see you.

Mrs. Merillia

Thank the Chancellor, and say that I have no desire for a dissolution at present, and shall do my best to prove worthy of my constitution.

Ferdinand (exiting)

Yes, ma'am.

Mrs. Merillia

I suppose it would not be feasible to station Gustavus at the telegraph office with a small hamper, so that he might collect the wires as they arrived and convey them here?

(Enter Ferdinand.)

Ferdinand

If you please, ma'am, Lady Postlethwaite is below, and asks if you are truly going, ma'am?

Mrs. Merillia

Going? Where to?

Ferdinand

The other place, ma'am. Her Ladyship is crying something terrible. She had no notion you was leaving so soon.

Mrs. Merillia

It is really very odd, so many people thinking—

(Enter Lady Enid.)

Enid

I am so shocked to hear the news. But, is it true that if anyone tapped on the door, you would certainly die? How can you be so sure of yourself?

Mrs. Merillia

What do you mean?

Enid

Why, there's a notice on the front door—

(Hennessey collapses.)

Mrs. Merillia (coolly)

You had better take death off the door, Mr. Ferdinand.

(Exit Mrs. Merillia.)

Ferdinand (exiting)

Yes, ma'am.

Enid

Why don't you have them sent to Jellybrand's?

Hennessey

Have what?

Enid (whispering with enormous satisfaction)

Your telegrams, (low) from your double life.

Hennessey

But, I assure you—

Enid

It's useless, really. I find you hidden away in Jellybrand's, drinking four-penny champagne with Mr. Sagittarius.—You told me you have secrets.

Hennessey

Did I?

Enid

Yes. When I said I'd guessed your secret you replied, "Which one?"

Hennessey

Oh.

Enid

You have strange guests. Then your grandmother is dying from the noise of the boys bringing the telegrams. And you tell me—me!—Minerva Partridge that you have no double life.

Hennessey

I suppose it is useless. Very well, my life is double.

Enid

So!

Hennessey

But only lately, quite lately.

Enid

Never mind that. You will soon get into it. Now, who is Mr. Sagittarius?

Hennessey

An acquaintance.

Enid

Well?

Hennessey

He's a man.

Enid

Then he's Malkiel. You can't deny it.

Hennessey

I can deny anything. I can and must.

Enid

Are you going to keep your promise to Mrs. Merillia and Sir Tiglath?

Hennessey

No.

Enid

I knew you wouldn't be able to.

Hennessey

Why?

Enid

Because when one has once been really and truly silly it's impossible to stop. Absolutely impossible. You'll go on, from one thing to another, as I do.

Hennessey

I cannot think that prophecy is silly.

Enid

You're worse than I am! It's splendid!

Hennessey

Worse!

Enid

Why, yes. You're foolish enough to think your acts sensible. I wish I could get to that.—Mr. Vivian, who do you think are the very silliest?

Hennessey

The anti-vaccinators.

Enid

No. They often get small pox and become quite sensible.

Hennessey

The atheists.

Enid

I used to think so, but not now. And most of the atheists I know are socialists at present. Every one knows socialists are very serious people.

Hennessey

Women who don't desire to be slaves?

Enid

There aren't any.

Hennessey

I give it up.

Enid

The spiritualists. That's why I love them best. How you would get on with them!

(Enter Ferdinand.)

Ferdinand

A gentleman and—uh—a lady to see you, sir.

Enid

I'm going. (whispering) I'll bet it's Malkiel. (exits

before Hennessey can do more than begin to deny it)

(Enter Malkiel and Mrs. Malkiel.)

Malkiel

You've nearly been the death of Madame, sir.

Hennessey

I'm sure I'm very sorry.

Malkiel

Sorrow is no salve, sir—no salve at all. Were it not for her books, I fear we might have lost her.

Hennessey

Good gracious!

Malkiel

Mercifully, her books comforted her. Madame is possessed of a magnificent library, sir; encyclopaedic in its scope and cosmopolitan in its point of view. In it are represented every age and every race since the dawn of letters; thousands upon thousands of authors. All bound in Persian calf. Among these she seeks solace. To these she flies in hours of anguish.

Hennessey

Does she indeed?

Malkiel

She desires to confer—and arrange measures for the protection of my life.—She is thinking out some problem, sir. She is communing with the mighty dead.—Sophronia, my love, Sophronia.

Mrs. Malkiel

I was immersed in thought. Thought matters, as Plato rightly observed.

Hennessey

Quite so.

Malkiel

Her whole knowledge comes straight from there.

Hennessey

Straight from there.

Mrs. Malkiel

What have you to say, Mr. Vivian? What is this danger that threatens my husband? And, what about rashes?

Malkiel

We'd better talk about the danger first, my dear.

Hennessey

Very well.

Mrs. Malkiel

Well, sir?

Hennessey

I thought it only right to warn you that I have learned there is a gentleman in London who has, for forty-five years, been seeking Malkiel with the avowed intention of—

Mrs. Malkiel

Of what, sir, of what?

Hennessey

Of doing him violence.

Malkiel

What is this gent's name?

Hennessey

That, I prefer not to say, at present.

Malkiel

But, why should he desire to?

Hennessey

Because you are a prophet.

Mrs. Malkiel

There! What have I always said. A prophet is always hated in his own country.

Malkiel

I know, my love, I know. But, how should he recognize me?

Hennessey

The gentleman has not recognized you. At the moment, he believes you are an American syndicate.

Malkiel

Thank mercy!

Hennessey (darkly)

But, one can never tell. He might find out.

Mrs. Malkiel

Nonsense! Don't be so timid.

Malkiel

Only cautious, Sophronia.

Mrs. Malkiel

I call a man who's afraid, even when he's passing as an American syndicate, a cowardly custard.—There, that's settled. So now, let us get to business. Before looking over your report, I wish to be made acquainted with those particulars.

Hennessey

Which ones?

Mrs. Malkiel

Those of your grandmother's career.

Malkiel

Let us take them in order. When was the old lady removed from the bottle?

Hennessey

Never! Never!

Mrs. Malkiel

Do you mean to tell me, she still sucks?

Hennessey

I mean what I say.

Malkiel

Well! She must be very partial to milk and rubber nipples.

Mrs. Malkiel

Her first tooth, Mr. Vivian? When did she cut it?

Hennessey

She has no idea.

Malkiel

Date of short-coating?

Hennessey

No date. She never wore a short coat.

Mrs. Malkiel

Do you desire me to believe that she has been going about in long clothes ever since she was born?

Hennessey

Most certainly, I do. She has always worn long clothes, and always will.

Mrs. Malkiel

Oh, very well. She must be a remarkable lady, that's all I can say. When did she put her hair up?

Hennessey

Never. She has never put it up.

Malkiel

You mean to say that your grandmother goes about in long clothes, with her hair down—in the central districts?

Hennessey

She has never put her hair up!

Mrs. Malkiel

Oh, well—if she prefers! But, I wonder what the police

are about—And now, the rashes?

Hennessey

None.

Mrs. Malkiel

Rubbish, Mr. Vivian. I must insist on knowing the number of rashes.

Hennessey

I assure you there are none.

Mrs. Malkiel

She's an unnatural old lady, that's all I can say. There's not many like her.

Hennessey

There is no one like her, no one at all.

Malkiel (stammering)

Well, and her—er—?

Mrs. Malkiel (all business, like a doctor)

Stop stammering like a school boy. Her period?

Hennessey

She—er—never had one.

Malkiel

What?

Mrs. Malkiel

Do you think we're fools—ignorant of elementary physiognomy?

Hennessey (wildly, obstinately)

She never had one! She's my grandmother! She never had one!

Mrs. Malkiel

Tell that to the Marines! What would Socrates have said in his oath?

CURTAIN

ACT IV
SCENE 7

A corridor in Hennessey Vivian's mansion leading to the dining room.

Hennessey and Mr. and Mrs. Malkiel enter.

Hennessey

If you tremble like that, of course, it must look too big. That's better, hold still. They won't notice anything odd. But, you've turned up Mr. Ferdinand's trousers.

Malkiel

They're too low.

Hennessey

They must cover the spats. Kindly turn them down.

Mrs. Malkiel

As to the spats, sir, the architects and their wives—

Hennessey

Mrs. Malkiel, I think it right to inform you, that if you mention the architects and their wives again, I may very probably go mad. (to Mr. Malkiel) Have the goodness to follow me, and to turn them down.—Remember, I shall introduce you as Mr. and Mrs. Sagittarius. (itching to strangle them) I wish to present you to my grandmother. My grandmother is not well, and conversation tires her. So, please, don't say too much in her presence. Only just now and then, you understand.

(Hennessey enters the dining room with the Malkiels.)

Hennessey

How do you do, Lady Postlethwaite? Grannie, I have persuaded my friends, Mr. and Madame Sagittarius—to join us at dinner. Sir Tiglath is most anxious to meet Mr. Sagittarius, who is a great astronomer. Let me—Mrs. Sagittarius, Mrs. Merillia, Mr. Sagittarius, Mrs. Merillia. Lady Julia Postlethwaite. Sir Tiglath. (they seat themselves)

Hennessey

I trust we shall have a pleasant spring this year.

Mrs. Malkiel

In the spring, the young man's fancy turns to thoughts of love. (silence) The Mouse is delicious in spring. Your

Ladyship, doubtless, loves the Mouse as I do.

Lady Julia

I am not specially fond of mice in spring, or indeed, at any season.

Mrs. Malkiel

I said the Mouse, your Ladyship. I observed that the Mouse was peculiarly delicious in the season of love.

Lady Julia

No mouse attracts me. I should much prefer spring to pass without the companionship of any mouse whatever.

(Enter Ferdinand.)

Sir Tiglath Butt.

(Mr. Sagittarius jumps up and upsets a vase of roses. Mrs. Merillia rises and shakes hands with Sir Tiglath.)

Mrs. Merillia

Let me introduce you. Sir Tiglath Butt. Mr. and Mrs. Sagittarius.

Tiglath (roaring)

Mr. Sagittarius—where is he? Ha—the old astronomer heard the name of Sagittarius. He has been informed that—

Malkiel

It's not true, sir, it's not true. I deny it. You are in error. I take the heavens to witness.

Tiglath

What do you mean, sir? And, why do you insult the heavens, you, an astronomer?

Malkiel

I am not an astronomer. I am an outside broker. I swear it. Sophronia, tell him!

Mrs. Malkiel

My husband states the fact. My husband brokes outside, and he has done so for the last twenty years.—Collect yourself, Jupiter.

Lady Julia

Pray, Mr. Vivian—tell me the worst—is he absolutely dangerous?

Hennessey

No, no. It's all his play.

Lady Julia

Play?

Hennessey

Yes. He's the most harmless, innocent creature. A child might stroke him. I mean, he wouldn't hurt a child.

Lady Julia

Yes, but we're not children.

Mrs. Malkiel

You are very pleasantly situated here, ma'am.

Mrs. Merillia

Yes, very pleasantly situated.

Mrs. Malkiel

It is, indeed, a blessing to be within easy reach of the stores.

Mrs. Merillia

The stores?

Mrs. Malkiel

Happy indeed, the good lady who dwells in the Central District.

Hennessey

Yes, Berkeley Square is very convenient in many ways.

Malkiel

Ah, the Berkeley Square. But, if you lived in the one behind Krummin's Mews, it would be quite another pair of boots, wouldn't it, ma'am?

Lady Julia

I'm sure he's dangerous, Mr. Vivian.

Mrs. Merillia

The one behind Krummin's Mews?

Malkiel

Aye, over against Brigwell's Buildings, just beyond the Pauper Lunatic Asylum.

Lady Julia

I daresay.

Mrs. Merillia

I am not acquainted with the neighborhood you mention.

Malkiel

You know the Mouse?

Mrs. Malkiel

Is your Ladyship to make one of the party at the Zoological Gardens tonight?

Lady Julia

Are you going to the Zoological Gardens?

Mrs. Malkiel

Yes, to an assembly. It should be very pleasant. Do you make one?

Lady Julia

I regret, I am not invited.

Mrs. Malkiel

Indeed! Yet, I presume your Ladyship is not insensible to the charms of roues and copulation?

Lady Julia

I beg your pardon?

Mrs. Malkiel

I imagine the social whirl finds you a willing acolyte?

Lady Julia

Oh, no. I go out very little.

Mrs. Malkiel

Indeed. Then, you do not frequent the palace?

Lady Julia

What do you mean?

Mrs. Malkiel

Buckingham Palace.

Lady Julia

I fear I don't catch your meaning.

Mrs. Malkiel

You are not an amicus curie?

Lady Julia

I am at sea.

Mrs. Malkiel

Does not your Ladyship comprehend the Latin tongue?

Lady Julia

Certainly not. Certainly not.

Mrs. Malkiel

Dear me! You hear her Ladyship, Jupiter?

Malkiel

I do, my angel.—Madame is a lady of deep learning.

Sir Tiglath

No decent female should understand Greek or Latin. If she does, she's sure to read a great deal she has no business to know.

Mrs. Malkiel

I beg to disagree, sir. In my opinion, the *Georgics* of Horatius, Homer's *Idylls*, and the satyrs of the great Juvenile—

Sir Tiglath

There never was a great Juvenile, ma'am. Talent must be mellow before it is worth the tasting. There never was and never will be a great Juvenile.—There can only be a juvenile preparing to be great.

Mrs. Malkiel (offended)

Really, sir!

Sir Tiglath

I affirm it, Madame. And, as you seem so mighty fond of Latin, remember what Horace said. Qui cupit opatum cursu continger metam. Multa tulit fecique puer, sudavit et alsit. (this finally shuts Mrs. Malkiel up) And now, sir, what's this about your being an outside broker? I was distinctly informed by this gentleman, only a day or two ago, that you were a distinguished astronomer.

Malkiel (horrified, to his wife)

I am betrayed! I said this was a trap. I said it was a rat-trap from the first.

Lady Julia

I knew he must be a rat-catcher. I was certain no one but a rat-catcher could behave in such a matter.

Hennessey

He is not indeed! Mr. Sagittarius, pray, sit down! You are alarming my grandmother.

Malkiel

I can't help that, sir. I am not going to sit here, sir, and be slain.

Hennessey

Tsh! Tsh! I merely informed Sir Tiglath that what Miss Minerva said about you was true.

Mrs. Malkiel

Miss Minerva? (jealously) Miss Minerva!

Hennessey

Lady Enid Thistle, I mean.

Mrs. Malkiel

Who's that?

Sir Tiglath

A young female who informed the old astronomer that your husband and a lady named Mrs. Bridgman had for a long while been carrying on—

Mrs. Malkiel

Carrying on! Jupiter!

Sir Tiglath

—astronomical investigations, and that they had come to the conclusion that there was probably oxygen in certain fixed stars.

Mrs. Malkiel

Jupiter, is this true?

Hennessey (aside to Malkiel)

Say yes, or he'll find out who you really are.

Malkiel

Yes.

Hennessey

Pray, Madame, pray—

Mrs. Malkiel

How can I pray here? You forget yourself.

Mrs. Merillia

Oh, Hennessey, what does this all mean?

Hennessey

Nothing, Grannie, nothing. Mr. Sagittarius is a very modest man.—Have an ice pudding.—Ferdinand, the ice pudding to Madame Sagittarius instantly!

Mrs. Malkiel

I cannot. At such a moment, food becomes repulsive.

Hennessey

I assure you, our cook's ice puddings are quite delicious. Aren't they, Grannie?

Mrs. Merillia

I have no idea, Hennessey.

Hennessey

Try it, Madame. I implore you, try it.

(Mrs. Malkiel politely does try it.)

Hennessey

Dear me! It's later than I had supposed. I am afraid we ought to be starting for the Zoological Gardens.

Malkiel

Certainly, sir, certainly. Mrs. Bridgman will be expecting us.

Mrs. Malkiel

I will assume my cloak, Jupiter.

Malkiel

My darling.

Mrs. Malkiel

Kindly, seek my furs.

Malkiel

Certainly, my love.

Sir Tiglath (rising)

The old astronomer will go with you.

Hennessey

I did not think you knew Mrs. Bridgman, Sir Tiglath?

Sir Tiglath

The old astronomer must know her before the evening is one more hour advanced.

Mrs. Merillia

Lady Julia, let us go upstairs.

Hennessey

Grannie, Lady Julia, I implore your forgiveness. Pardon me.

Mrs. Merillia

Oh, Julia, you were a lady-in-waiting to Her Majesty.—Tell me what it all means.

Lady Julia (solemnly)

Victoria—it means your grandson has fallen into the clutches of a most dangerous and determined rat-catcher.

CURTAIN

ACT IV
SCENE 8

The Bridgman Mansion. Mrs. Malkiel, dragging Mr. Malkiel, is knocking on the door.

Mrs. Malkiel

Is this the habitation of the woman Bridgman?

Malkiel

My darling, my love, I swear upon the infant head of Capricornus that Mrs. Bridgman and I—

Mrs. Malkiel

Enough! Be sure that I will inquire into this matter further.

Hennessey

Mr. Vivian is my name. I think Miss Minerva mentioned to you—

Mrs. Bridgman

Of course. You are to be kind enough to introduce me to Mr. Sadg—something or other, and I am to introduce him to Sir Tiglath Butt, when Sir Tiglath Butt has been introduced to me by Miss Partridge. It is all to work out beautifully. Yes, yes, charming! Charming.

Hennessey

I have ventured to bring Mr. and Madame Sagittarius with me tonight.

Mrs. Bridgman

Delighted! Delighted! How d'you do, Mr. Sagittarius?

Mr. Biggle (who is standing near Hennessey)

Biggle! Biggle! Biggle!

Mrs. Bridgman

Yes indeed, I so agree with you, dear Mr. Sagittarius.

Biggle

Biggle! Biggle! Biggle!

Mrs. Bridgman (to Hennessey)

What does he mean? How does one biggle?

Hennessey

I think that is his name.

Mrs. Bridgman (elegant hostess that she is, realizing and covering her mistake)

Biggle—of course. Delighted to see you—Ah, Mr. Sagi—I have heard so much about you from dear Miss Minerva.

Malkiel

My loved and honored wife, a lady of deep education.

Mrs. Bridgman

Delighted.

Mrs. Malkiel

It is, indeed, time that this encounter took place. Henceforth, ma'am, I shall be ever at my husband's side—ma'am.

Mrs. Bridgman (not paying the slightest attention)

So glad. I have been longing for this.

Footman

Mr. Bernard Wilkins!

Mrs. Malkiel

The prophet from the Risel.

Footman

Mrs. Eliza Doubleway.

Mrs. Malkiel

Mrs. Eliza! That's the soothsayer from the Beck.

Footman

Professor Elijah Chapman.

Malkiel

The nose-reader from the Downs. We are in it tonight. We are indeed; we are fairly and squarely in our element.

Mrs. Malkiel

They needn't think to come over me.—(to a guest who has walked on her train) Don't set your feet on me, sir, if you please.

Footman

Mr. Amos Towle.

Malkiel

The great medium from the Wick.

Mrs. Malkiel

The celebrated Towle.

Malkiel

The one and only Towle.

Mrs. Malkiel

We must—we must see Towle.

Malkiel

Oh, where is Towle?

Mrs. Bridgman

Oh, Mr. Towle—delighted. How sweet of you to come out all this way from your eyrie at the Wick. You'll find many friends—Miss Minerva—your greatest admirer and disciple.

Enid (in her persona as Miss Minerva)

Oh, Mr. Vivian, I'm glad you've come! Let me introduce you to my great friend, Eureka, and Mr. Briskin.

Briskin

Pretty sight. All these little dears enjoying themselves so innocently. Mother Bridgman's chickens. But, it's impossible to count them even after they've hatched. Cheese it!

Footman

Sir?

Briskin

Cheese it! Anything for me tonight, Eureka? Anything lucky? Give us a chance, mother!

Eureka

I do see something. It's just close to you on that table.

Briskin

My word, my word, mother. What's the blessed little symbol like?

Eureka

You must wait a moment. It's not clear. It's all cloudy.

Briskin

Been imbibing, mother? Has the blessed little symbol

been at it, again?

Eureka

It's getting clearer.—Ah—now, it steps out. It's got a hump.

Briskin

Is it a camel?

Eureka

It's a rhinoceros. It's moving to you.

Briskin

What's it mean, mother?

Eureka

It's a sign of plenty.

Briskin

Plenty.

Eureka

Good fortune, because its head is toward you. If it had presented its tail, it would mean black weather.

Briskin

Don't let it turn tail. (drinking a brandy) Ha! Got him!

Enid

D'you see anything for Mr. Vivian, Eureka?

Eureka

Something right around his head.

Enid

Is it a halo?

Eureka

No—some form of bird.

Briskin

I heard the owl 'neath the eaves complaining. Is it an owl, mother? Ask it to screech.

Hennessey (scared)

What does it mean?

Eureka

Oh, you're all right. I'm tired. Somebody get me a drink.

Briskin

Mother's peckish.—Waiter!

Waiter

Sir?

Briskin

This lady's so peckish, she could swallow anything. Bring her anything, will you? Trot, boy, trot!

Hennessey (to Miss Minerva/Enid)

Sir Tiglath's coming.

Eureka

I'm going to the buffet.

Enid

Do eat something. All this second sight takes something out of you.

Briskin

Mother Eureka's so hungry she'd even eat oats.

Enid (to Hennessey)

Sir Tiglath coming here? But, he doesn't know Mrs.

Bridgman.

Hennessey

I know—but he's coming. And, not only that, but Mr. and Mrs. Sagittarius are here already.

Enid

I see—I see.

Hennessey

What—not the sparrow on my head?

Enid

No. But, I see that you're taking your double life in real earnest.

Hennessey

I?

Enid

Yes. Now, that's all very well—and you know, I'm the last person to complain of anything of the sort, so long as it doesn't get me into difficulties.

Hennessey

And, what about the difficulties you've got me in?

Enid

Well, I'm sure I've done nothing—

Hennessey

Nothing! You made me come here, and insisted I bring Mr. Sagittarius, and—

Enid

Oh well, that's nothing. But, Sir Tiglath mustn't see me here as Miss Minerva. Has he arrived yet?

Hennessey

I don't think so.

Enid

Good. Run outside, and persuade him to go home, when he gets here.

Hennessey

I am grieved to declare that I cannot contend physically with Sir Tiglath.

Enid

Who asked you to contend physically?

Hennessey

Nothing but personal violence will keep Sir Tiglath from coming here.

Enid

Hmm! What's to be done?—I know! I'll masquerade as myself.

Hennessey

As yourself?

Enid

Yes. You see, everyone here knows I've got an astral body—

Hennessey

I've always said you were lovely, Enid.

Enid

No, no. It's a sort of floating business. I've told everybody Lady Enid Thistle is a sort of ancestress of mine—and her astral body appears sometimes.

Hennessey

Why did you?

Enid

Because it was so idiotic.

Hennessey

I see. Why didn't I think of that?

Enid

Ah, Eureka, darling, do I look odd? I suddenly began to feel astral—just as I was having my drink.—I can't help thinking that Lady Enid, you know, my ancestress, who's always with me—is peculiarly powerful tonight.

Briskin

Watch out for the hump, mother.

Eureka

I see you! You are astral! You are Lady Enid emerged for an hour from our dear Minerva.

Enid

I thought so. I thought so. Because, when someone

called me Miss Minerva just now, I felt angry. Tell them, dear Eureka—tell all my friends of your discovery.

(Enter Harriet.)

Harriet

My blessing! Miss Minerva!

Enid

Lady Enid, Harriet love, tonight. Eureka says I'm astral.

Harriet

Oh, Mr. Towle, will you materialize for us tonight?

Mrs. Bridgman

Yes, yes. He's promised to—after supper.

Enid

How delightful! Mr. Towle, tell me, do you agree with Eureka? Am I astral?

Towle

As like as not. Astral, that's it. Astral to a "T".

Enid

Then I'm Lady Enid Thistle, my ancestress, who's always with me?

Towle

Aye, aye! Every bit of her! Her Ladyship to a "T".

Voices

It's Lady Enid—in the astral plane.

Footman (bawling out)

Sir Tiglath Butt.

Mrs. Bridgman

So glad! So enchanted! Just a few interesting people.

Sir Tiglath

What, Madame? So, you're the brain and the eye, eh? Is that it?

Mrs. Bridgman

Ah, yes, indeed! The brain and I, Sir Tiglath, so good of you to say so!

Sir Tiglath

You prompted his interest in the holy stars? You drove him to the telescope; you told him to clear up the matter, did you?

Mrs. Bridgman (puzzled out of being a perfect hostess)

What matter?

Enid

Say the oxygen, darling.

Hennessey

Say the oxygen.

Mrs. Bridgman (recovering)

Oh, yes, Sir Tiglath, I told him—to make quite sure.

Sir Tiglath

And, your original adviser was Mr. Sagittarius, was he?

Mrs. Bridgman

Mr. Sagittarius,—ah, yes. Sir Tiglath is speaking of you, Mr. Saji—

(Mrs. Bridgman turns to Mr. Biggle.)

Biggle

Biggle! Biggle! Biggle!

Enid

By the way, where is Mr. Sagittarius? I haven't seen him yet.

Mrs. Bridgman

I'm afraid he's angry with me. (crushed) I really can't think why.

Enid

Sir Tiglath, come with me. I want you to find Mr. Sagittarius for me.

Towle (looking at Sir Tiglath's hand)

Tremendous! Very big. You've got a very spatulate hand there, sir,—allow me? (trying to read his palm)

Sir Tiglath

How dare you tamper with the old astronomer, sir? Who are all these crazy Janes? Drop my hand, sir.

Mrs. Malkiel (to her husband)

We have only to declare ourselves to be received as royalty.

Malkiel (fearful)

But—

Mrs. Malkiel

Declare yourself, Jupiter. Declare yourself this moment!

Malkiel

My love, my angel, we must reflect.

Mrs. Malkiel

I have reflected.

Malkiel

There are difficulties, my dear, many difficulties in the way.

Mrs. Malkiel

And, what if there are? Every fool knows that.

Malkiel

My dear, you are a little hard upon me.

Mrs. Malkiel

And, what have you been upon me, I should like to know? What about those goings on with the woman Bridgman?—And this hussy Minerva? You've been her owl—that's what you've been.

Malkiel

My love, I've told you. I have sworn.

Mrs. Malkiel

What man doesn't swear when he gets the chance? (sobbing) Why did I ever marry?

Malkiel

My angel—be calm!

Mrs. Malkiel

Very well, then. Declare yourself, Jupiter, this minute or I'll declare yourself for you!

Malkiel

But, my love, think of Sir Tiglath! I dare not declare myself. He will be here at any moment—and he has sworn to kill me.

Mrs. Malkiel

Rubbish!

Malkiel

But my—

Mrs. Malkiel

Rubbish! That's only what Mr. Vivian says.

Malkiel

Well, but—

Mrs. Malkiel

You could knock him down.—It's no use talking to me, Jupiter.

Malkiel

I know it isn't, my darling, I know, but—

Mrs. Malkiel

You just don't want to do it! I will not endure to be left in a corner while all these nobodies are being truckled to. Bernard Wilkins, indeed! A prophet we don't so much as recognize as a prophet. It's downright disgusting, and I won't have it.

Enid

There you are!

Mrs. Malkiel (storming off)

Very well, Jupiter, since you won't declare yourself, I shall go at once to the woman Bridgman, and declare yourself for you.

Enid

Dear me, Mr. Sagittarius, is your wife going to make a declaration? This is most interesting. Excuse me, Sir Tiglath, I'll be back in a moment.

(Enid goes off, leaving Sir Tiglath with Mr. Malkiel who is visibly terrified.)

Sir Tiglath

Is this a madhouse? The old astronomer demands to know at once.

Malkiel

I don't know, sir. Indeed, I should not like to express an opinion on the point. If you will excuse—?

Sir Tiglath

The old astronomer will not excuse you. He will not be

run away from by everybody in this manner.

Malkiel (lying shamelessly)

I beg pardon, sir, I had no intention of running away.

Sir Tiglath

Then, why did you do it, sir? Tell the old astronomer that? And tell him, moreover, what you and the female Bridgman have been about together?

Malkiel (horrified)

Nothing, sir. I swear that Mrs. Bridgman and myself have never—

Sir Tiglath

Never made investigations?

Malkiel (indignant)

What do you take me for?

Sir Tiglath

Do you affirm that you are no astronomer, sir?

Malkiel

I do! I do!

Sir Tiglath

Modest and retiring?

Malkiel

That's it. I'm a modest and retiring outside broker.

Sir Tiglath

There never was a modest and retiring outside broker! There never was and there never will be. The old astronomer—

Voices

The prophet from the Mouse—

Malkiel

What's that? Whatever's that?

Voices

The Great Malkiel—the greatest prophet of the age. He's here—

Sir Tiglath (having found the foe at last)

Malkiel, Malkiel—who has insulted the holy stars! Here! Where? (craftily) Where is he?

Malkiel (pointing)

In there, I believe!

Sir Tiglath (in a menacing way, like a lion stalking his prey)

Let me find him! Let me only discover him! I'll break every bone in his accursed body.

(Malkiel, freed at last of Sir Tiglath, runs out to the right.)

Mrs. Malkiel (entering from the left, leading the crowd)

Oh, Jupiter, where are you?

CURTAIN

ACT V
SCENE 9

Hennessey Vivian's mansion again.

Malkiel comes in hurriedly and speaks to Gustavus.

Malkiel (confidentially)

You know me?

Gustavus

Yes, sir. By the clothes. I should know Mr. Ferdinand's trouserings in a thousand.

Malkiel

Right. I have returned to change them.

Gustavus

Yes, sir. Mr. Ferdinand has retired to bed, sir.

Malkiel

Don't wake him. I can just leave them for him.

Gustavus

Very well, sir.

Malkiel

What is your name, young man?

Gustavus

Gustavus, sir.

Malkiel

Ah, Gustavus, would you like to earn a pound?

Gustavus

I don't say as how I'd rather not, sir.

Malkiel

Right! Right! Do as I tell you, and you'll earn a pound.

Gustavus

I'll do it, sir. What do you want me to do?

Malkiel

First, let me change clothes, then hide me somewhere, so I can sleep. First light, call me—and—I shall be off to the docks.

Gustavus

The docks?

Malkiel

Ah, I start for Java tomorrow. Now, let me change clothes. They're in Mr. Vivian's room, aren't they?

Gustavus

You must go soft, sir, because of the old lady. She's been awful upset.

Malkiel

I'll go as soft as a mouse. Show me the way.

Mrs. Merillia (calling)

Hennessey! Hennessey!

(Gustavus and Mr. Malkiel stop in their tracks.)

Mrs. Merillia

Hennessey! Come in here. I must speak to you, Hennessey. (coming in with her cane) Eeek! The rat-catcher! The rat-catcher!

Malkiel

Hide me, hide me.

(Enter Fancy.)

Fancy

Oh, Mr. Gustavus! Is it the robbers again? Is it murder, Mr. Gustavus? Is it fire?

Gustavus

I don't know, Mrs. Fancy. I'll ask the mistress.

Mrs. Merillia (blockading herself behind the door)

You can't come in! You can't come in, and if you do, I shall give you in charge to the police.

Fancy

Ma'am! Ma'am!

Mrs. Merillia

It's no use your knocking. The door is bolted. Go away! Go away!

Fancy

Madame! Madame! It's me.

Mrs. Merillia

I know it's you! I saw you! Leave the house, unless you wish to be at once put in prison.

Fancy

Me to leave the house! Me to go to prison!

Gustavus

Bear up, Mrs. Fancy. She doesn't know who it is!

Mrs. Merillia

I am ringing. I am summoning assistance. You will be captured if you don't go away.

Gustavus

Lord—I hear Mr. Vivian. Here's a nice go.

Hennessey (entering)

What's that?

Gustavus

I think it's Mrs. Merillia, sir. She keeps on ringing.

Hennessey

At this hour? Is she ill?

Gustavus

I don't know, sir. She keeps ringing, but when I answer it, she says "Go away".

Hennessey

Strange!

Mrs. Merillia

If you try to break in, you will be put in prison at once. I hear assistance coming. I hear the police. Go away, you wicked, wicked man.

Hennessey

Grannie! Grannie, let me in! Grannie! Grannie! Don't ring! Grannie! Grannie!

Mrs. Merillia

It's useless for you to say that. I know who you are. I saw you. I shall go on ringing as long as I stand. I shall die ringing, but I shall never let you in. Go away! Go away!

Hennessey

What does she mean?

Gustavus

I can't say, indeed, sir.

Hennessey

Grannie! Grannie!

Mrs. Merillia

I am heating the poker! If you come in, you will repent it. I am heating the poker.

Hennessey

This is a matter for me alone. Mrs. Fancy, please go away at once. Gustavus, you will accompany Mrs. Fancy.

Mrs. Merillia

I can hear you. I hear you breathing. The poker is red hot.

Hennessey

Grannie, dearest Grannie.

Mrs. Merillia

I dare you to come in.

Hennessey

I'm not coming in, Grannie.

Mrs. Merillia

Then, go away, and let me hear you going.

(Hennessey goes out noisily and enters again quietly after a moment.)

Hennessey

Grannie, are you ringing?

Mrs. Merillia (coming out)

Oh, Hennessey! Hennessey!

Hennessey

Grannie, what is it?

Mrs. Merillia

The rat-catcher! The rat-catcher!

Hennessey

The rat-catcher?

Mrs. Merillia

He has come back. He is here. He has been trying to break into my room.

Hennessey

What rat-catcher?

Mrs. Merillia

Mr. Sagittarius.

Hennessey

He is here?

Mrs. Merillia

I have seen him. He has tried to murder me.

Hennessey

I will look into this at once. Gustavus!

Gustavus (entering)

Sir?

Hennessey

Has Mr. Sagittarius returned?

Gustavus

No, sir.

Hennessey

Has anybody entered the house?

Gustavus

No, sir.

Hennessey

Grannie, you hear what Gustavus says?

Mrs. Merillia

But, Hennessey, he is here. I saw him.

Hennessey

Grannie, it must have been a dream.

Mrs. Merillia

No, Hennessey, no.

Hennessey

But, I left him at Mrs. Bridgman's.

Mrs. Merillia

But, I saw him here with my own eyes.

Hennessey

At any rate, I'm here now. Nothing can hurt you.

(Hennessey leads Mrs. Merillia out. The lights dim, then go up. As the lights go up, Mrs. Malkiel enters with Gustavus.)

Mrs. Malkiel

What do you mean, young man? Where is my husband?

Gustavus

Ma'am?

Mrs. Malkiel

Where, I say, is my husband?

Gustavus

I can't say, I'm sure, ma'am. Mrs. Merillia and Mr. Vivian are not at home.

Mrs. Malkiel

Then, all I can say is they ought to be at home at this time of night. Are you aware that Mr. Vivian has invited me to stay the night here?

Gustavus

No, ma'am.

Mrs. Malkiel

That'll do. If I have any more of your impertinence, I'll make you repent of it. You are evidently not aware of who I am. (enter Hennessey) What! Mr. Vivian!

Hennessey

Hush! For mercy sakes, hush! My grandmother.

Mrs. Malkiel

Is a fidgety old lady. Although you do tell a parcel of

lies about her.

Hennessey

Lies!

Mrs. Malkiel

Yes, lies. She don't wear long clothes.

Hennessey

I beg your pardon?

Mrs. Malkiel

She don't wear her hair down. She don't have her period. Foh! Lies, all lies! Where is my husband?

Hennessey

I have no idea. I regret to say that I must conduct you to your carriage. My grandmother is seriously indisposed, and I myself need rest.

Mrs. Malkiel

Well then, you can't have it.

Hennessey

I beg your pardon? I really regret that I must retire.

Allow me—

Mrs. Malkiel

I will not allow you. Where is my husband?

Hennessey

He has probably returned home.

Mrs. Malkiel

To the Mouse? Then, he's a coward, and an oath-breaker. If Sir Tiglath were to catch him, I shouldn't feel sorry.—Very well, lead me at once to the telescope.

Hennessey

What for?

Mrs. Malkiel

Did we not come here to go into the dressed Crab?

Hennessey

I really cannot, without a chaperone—

Mrs. Malkiel

Stuff! The wife of Malkiel needs no chaperone.

Hennessey

Very well, Mrs. Malkiel. But, I really think such a proceeding will cause a grave scandal to the Square.

Mrs. Malkiel

What is the Square to me, or I to the Square?

Hennessey

What do you wish me to do?

Mrs. Malkiel

Proceed at once to your investigation.

Hennessey

I am in no condition.

Mrs. Malkiel

It is useless to talk, Mr. Vivian.

Hennessey

But, your husband—

Mrs. Malkiel

My husband is a coward, unworthy of such a wife as he possesses.

(Noise off.)

Mrs. Malkiel

What was that?

Hennessey

Rats, I have no doubt.

Mrs. Malkiel

Rats or no rats, I intend to see this matter out. The night wanes. Kindly go at once to the telescope.

Hennessey

Really, I—

Mrs. Malkiel

Have the goodness to place the old lady in the claws of the Crab.

Hennessey (pulling out the telescope and looking out the window through it)

I really can't find the Crab. I see the Great Bear.

Mrs. Malkiel

That is no use. The Bear has nothing to do with the old

lady. You must find the Crab. Look again.

Hennessey

There is no Crab tonight. I assure you, on my honor, there is none.

(A bell rings.)

Hennessey

Merciful heavens! Who can that be? Grannie must not be disturbed.

Mrs. Malkiel

Do you think that can be my husband? I shouldn't like him to—Do you think it's him?

Hennessey (going to the door)

I will very soon see.

(Lady Enid enters. Sir Tiglath is right behind her.)

Enid

I thought you'd be here, Mr. Vivian.

Sir Tiglath

Where is he? Where is he?

Enid

Sir Tiglath means Malkiel. He is most anxious to meet him. I rather think Sir Tiglath wishes to try if he can murder Malkiel. Do you think he can bring it off?

Hennessey

I'm sure I don't know. Good night.

Enid

But, we want to come in.

Sir Tiglath

Young man, the old astronomer will not leave this house until he has searched it from cellar to attic.

Hennessey

I'm sorry, but you can't. If you wish to murder Malkiel, I shall not prevent you, but he is not here.

Enid

Then, where is he?

Hennessey

I don't know.

Enid

Malkiel's in the house and Gustavus knows it.

Gustavus (rushing in)

Oh, sir, forgive me! He only wanted to change his clothes, before he went off to Java.

Sir Tiglath

To where?

Gustavus

To Java, sir.

Hennessey

Then, he is in the house?

Gustavus (evasively)

Well, sir, he was. And I ain't seen him go.

Hennessey

Sir Tiglath, you can enter. My grandmother was right.

Sir Tiglath

Right about what?

Hennessey

She told me that the ruffian was in the house, and had attempted to make away with her.

Enid

Dear me, this is most interesting.

Hennessey

I thought she was dreaming. You can search the house, and if you find him, murder him at once. I hope you will find him.

Sir Tiglath

Why?

Hennessey

Because I think it quite time that he was murdered. You may search anywhere but my grandmother's bedroom. When you have found the ruffian, and murdered him, I shall be glad to hear your news.

(Hennessey pulls out a Police whistle, goes to the door and blows it shrilly. After a moment a Bobby runs up.)

Hennessey

Officer.

Bobby

Suh!

Hennessey

Stand there by the gate, and if anyone should run out, knock him down with your truncheon.

Bobby (off)

Yes, sir.

Hennessey (closing the door)

Lady Enid, you have heard what this villain is doing here, and you must be sensible. You can have no part in the search.

Enid (protesting)

Oh, but I particularly want—

Hennessey (gravely)

You must retire. Fancy will look after you.

Enid

Really, Mr. Vivian—

Hennessey (imperious)

Kindly, follow me.

Enid (Following him meekly, but against her will)

Can't I really—

Hennessey

Certainly not. If you were a married woman, possibly—

Enid (brightly)

But I'm engaged.

Hennessey (stupefied)

Engaged! To whom?

Enid

Sir Tiglath.

Hennessey

Why?

Enid

Because he didn't find out I'm Miss Minerva, and he must never know. Besides, I always wanted him to propose to me.

Hennessey (baffled)

I'll never understand women. Why?

Enid

Because I thought it would be supremely idiotic for me to accept him.

Hennessey (not wishing to hear any more for fear that madness lies this way)

To be sure. Of course. Come with me. (seeing Fancy emerge unsteadily from a side room) Please guard this young lady.

Fancy (clinging to Enid desperately)

Oh, yes. Protect. Guard.

(Fancy and Enid go into a side room, but it's not clear who is protecting whom.)

Hennessey

Now Sir Tiglath you may proceed.

(Sir Tiglath remains immobile.)

Hennessey

I hope you will find him.

Sir Tiglath (still motionless)

Why?

Hennessey

Because I think it quite time he was murdered. (imperiously) Begin.

Sir Tiglath (not moving but looking apprehensively in all directions)

Where is the old astronomer to search?

Hennessey

Anywhere except my Grandmother's bedroom. Those precincts are sacred. BEGIN!

Sir Tiglath (terrified)

I'm going to. The old astronomer does not know the meaning of fear.

(Sir Tiglath's knees knock. The clock strikes two. Sir Tiglath jumps and clasps Gustavus who would like to run away, but cannot.)

Hennessey (implacably)

Begin.

Sir Tiglath

The old astronomer must have a (stammering) c'c'candle!

Hennessey

Here is one.

Sir Tiglath

L'le'lighted.

Hennessey

Ah, of course, so you can see your victim to murder him. (solemnly) Gustavus, light the candle.

(Shaking like a leaf, Gustavus cannot do it. With remarkable calm, Hennessey lights the candle.)

Hennessey

There. Begin.

Sir Tiglath: You will a'c'company the old a'as'stronomer?

Hennessey

No. I will rest here. When you've found him and murdered him, I shall be glad to hear the manner in which he was slain.

(Hennessey sits down comfortably and picks up a magazine, nonchalantly flipping through it. Slowly, like a man proceeding to his doom and grasping Gustavus in an iron death grip, Sir Tiglath proceeds upstairs. Sir Tiglath and Gustavus vanish. After a moment there is a noise of glass breaking. Then a huge thud. Then screaming. Hennessey continues to read with the utmost calm and puts his feet up on the puff. Suddenly Mrs. Malkiel emerges running, disheveled, her husband in hot pursuit. She runs upstairs. Malkiel follows her, but can't quite catch her. Hennessey continues to read without taking any notice. Silence. Then there is a loud rapping at the door.)

Hennessey (without looking up)

Gustavus. (no response) Gustavus! (no response, the rapping gets louder) Annoying. (pained, he goes to the door and opens it himself) Well?

Bobby (entering and dragging in the unconscious Sir Tiglath and depositing him unceremoniously on the couch like a used rag)

I knocked this bloke down as he was trying to escape.

Hennessey

Indeed.

(Screaming is heard from the Malkiels upstairs.)

Bobby (looking upstairs)

Let's nab 'em!

Hennessey

You think it would be wise to—what was the word you used?

Bobby

Nab 'em!

Hennessey

Yes. Would it be wise to do so?

Bobby

What else am I here for?

Hennessey

Oh, well, then, by all means nab 'em. I shall not prevent you.

(The Bobby rushes upstairs brandishing his truncheon. More screaming. More glass breaking. Hennessey goes to the fire-place and warms his hands.)

Bobby (returning with Mrs. Merillia in a black gown)

Here's one of 'em. (Before Hennessey can turn to protest, he's thrust her into his arms and is on his way back upstairs.) You keep an eye on that old bird while I fetch the rest. I'M COMING!!!

Hennessey (horrified)

Grannie! Grannie!

Mrs. Merillia

Don't ever call me your Grannie again! Oh. (she faints dead away.)

Hennessey (leaning over his grandmother, trying to resuscitate her)

Grandmother! Speak to me! Speak to me!

(The Malkiels rush out, pursuing each other, pursued by the Policeman, who trips and falls as the Curtain falls.

CURTAIN

ABOUT THE AUTHOR

Frank J. Morlock has written and translated many plays since retiring from the legal profession in 1992. His translations have also appeared on Project Gutenberg, the Alexandre Dumas Père web page, Literature in the Age of Napoléon, Infinite Artistries.com, and Munsey's (formerly Blackmask). In 2006 he received an award from the North American Jules Verne Society for his translations of Verne's plays. He lives and works in México.

www.ingramcontent.com/pod-product-compliance
Lightning Source LLC
LaVergne TN
LVHW041619070426
835507LV00008B/338